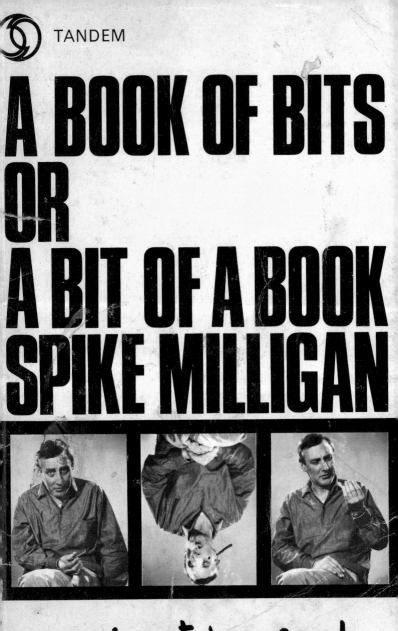

TANDEM

A BOOK OF BITS
OR
A BIT OF A BOOK
SPIKE MILLIGAN

its here at last folks!

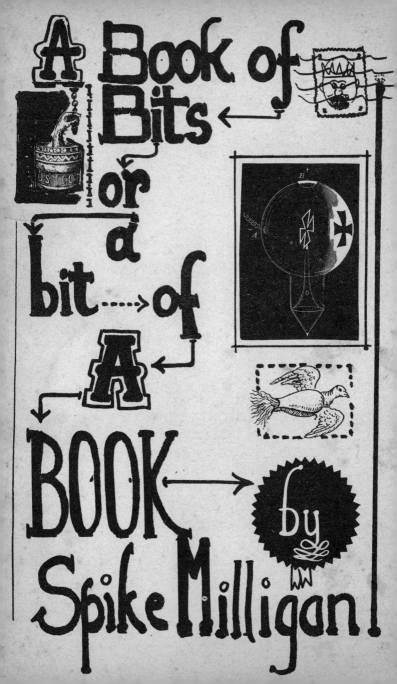

A Book of Bits ← or a bit .....of A BOOK → by Spike Milligan!

HAIRY WADING TWITTS.

PLUCKED HAIRES. TWYT

A Book of Bits

A Book of Bits

or

A Bit of A Book

by

Spike Milligan

TANDEM
14 Gloucester Road, London SW7

First published in 1965 Dennis Dobson Ltd.

Copyright © Spike Milligan 1965

Tandem edition published by
Universal-Tandem Publishing Co. Ltd., 1967
Reprinted May 1968
Reprinted January 1969
Reprinted November 1970
Reprinted October 1971
Reprinted July 1972
Reprinted February 1973

Pull Down St. Paul's! first appeared in *The Observer*
Agent 008 first appeared in *Private Eye*

Printed in Great Britain by The Anchor Press Ltd.,
and bound by Wm. Brendon & Son Ltd.,
both of Tiptree, Essex

DEDICATION

This book is dedicated to The Family Planning International Save the Wildlife Fund and President J. Nyerere of Tanzania for his enlightened attitude towards the preservation of his country's fauna.

CONTENTS

Bit One
SQUARE BITS
13

Bit Two
SIMPLE VERSE
FOR
SIMPLE TONS
31

Bit Three
TWIT BITS
53

Bit Four
SO-SO STORIES
63

Bit Five
DENSE JUNGLE
FOR
DENSE PEOPLE
81

Bit One
SQUARE BITS

You cannot hear what he is playing as this is a
silent film.

Coat of Arms
of
King Size II

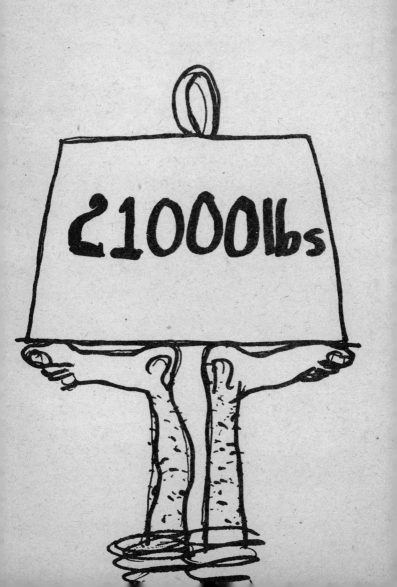

"Believe me, darling, when he's made into a meat pie you won't be able
to tell the difference."

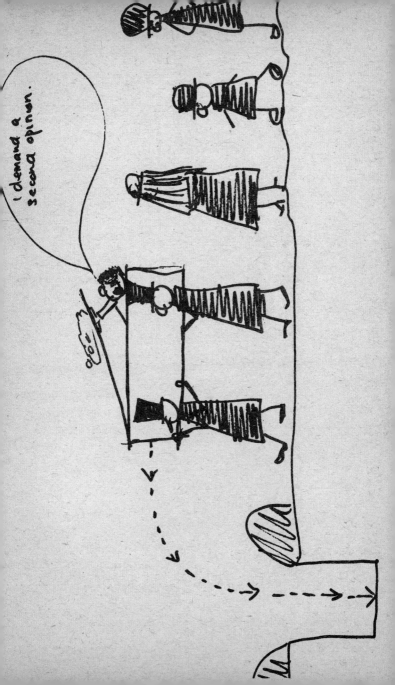

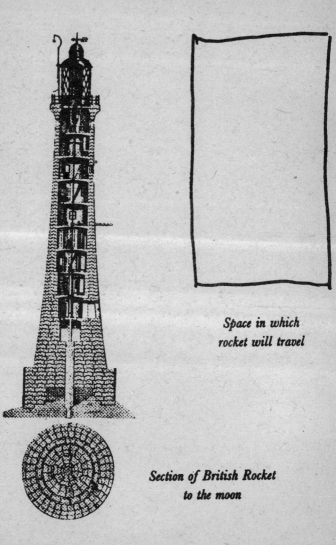

Space in which
rocket will travel

Section of British Rocket
to the moon

*British rocket
being fired*

*Squadron Leader Martin-Twinnick,
the pilot, waving goodbye for ever*

" _____ "

Fill in caption under picture. If satisfied with result,
award yourself 3 points and shout "Hooray!" twice.

New Oil Process

Sent on **7 days'** Free Trial.

Gaby Desleys

Render yourself unconscious in the privacy of your own room!

"I can see right up your nose."

"And it's cheaper than Pal."

"The bath attendant never said anything about this."

HOW TO AVOID NATIONAL SERVICE DURING A WAR

Exercises to be performed before an army medical board.

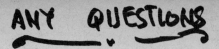

The Boy's Own Paper.

Correspondence.

I.—SOME FINGER TRICKS.

WHY sit and twiddle your thumbs when you have an unoccupied moment? This is not a riddle, but a plain, straightforward question.

You will probably answer, thumb-twiddling is not your habit. Quite right, too, it is an idiotic practice, that any duffer can accomplish. Try twiddling your hands, only in the reverse way, and you will have a task that will cost you some pains to accomplish successfully. I don't say you will have effected much when you have succeeded, beyond a strengthening of your will power, but, at any rate, you will have prevented your hands from being idle, and consequently, according to Dr. Watts, you will have escaped a temptation to indulge in mischief, and this in the case of some boys is no small matter.

Fig. 1 will show you the position your hands are to take on starting. With the index finger of the right you are to describe a circle in the air *towards* you, or as shown in the direction by the arrow, while with the index finger of the left hand you at the same time describe a circle *away* from you. To do this easily and without apparent effort will take long practice, and a severe mental struggle, for it is surprising how determined the two hands seem to be to follow each other. But, for your encouragement, I may say that it *is* to be accomplished, and some boys will find the task easier than others. The hands are drawn as seen by their owner.

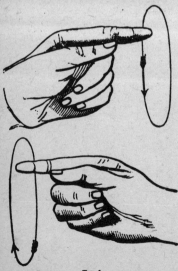

FIG. 1.

AMICUS (Bedford).—You must not be frightened by every old wife's tale that is told you. Just try to recall the names of all the professional ventriloquists you have ever heard of, and consider how many of them died young of chest complaint ! Straining of all kinds, whether of lungs or legs, is doubtless bad, but then exercise is equally good.

A SLAVE (Repentant).—You must get free first, then consult a doctor *boldly*. Your physique cannot be good if the memory is gone.

S. MASON.—To stop the squeaking of the boots, make a few holes in the soles with a fine bradawl, and stand them for a night in a plate of castor oil, or any vegetable oil.

DISFIGUREMENT OF NOSE (A. D. McCushie).—Try snuffing up a little hazeline morning and night. Wear gloves if you cannot help picking it

RABBIT (E. A. M.).—Change his hutch at once. Give plenty of good grain, not much green food. Keep warm and dry. We fear he will die, however.

BAD HABITS (S. F. R.).—You are killing yourself by inches.

DOG AND MUSIC (R. C. M.).—Let her enjoy herself.

GOING TO BED (W. L. P.).—A boy of thirteen should go to bed at 8 or 9 o'clock, and rise at 7 ; take his bath, and go out for a stroll before breakfast. If you do so, you will have a chance to grow up a man.

NITS (Primrose).—Any druggist will give you a wash.

W. P.—There is no time like now. Now is the best time to join the Navy ; now is the best time to do anything to which you have made up your mind. Go to the east end of the National Gallery at ten o'clock in the morning and ask the man-o'-war's man.

TONSILS (Anxious).—Silly. Everybody has them.

DONALD.—We are sorry you are so weak in your understanding, but we do not know of a special knee-flattener or calf-extender. We can quite understand that a mere "shaver" in a kilt may feel uncomfortable, particularly if he is thinking of his knees and calves all the time, but if he were to think of something else the discomfort would probably be alleviated. More to eat, more exercise, and more unconsciousness, might help you to laugh and grow fat ; and if it did not it would not matter much.

A. and M. W. FORBES.—"Kentish Fire" is a method of clapping hands, with three claps and a pause, keeping time, instead of applauding with an irregular and general clapping.

How to point round corners.

Bit Two

SIMPLE VERSE
FOR
SIMPLE TONS

"Oh, all right then. I'll marry you."

CASABAZONKA

The boy stood on
the burning deck
Whence all but
he had fled -

Twit.

Chorus- Rule Britannia etc

TWIT

BURN

BURN

SCORCH

SEA-LEGS?

ANCIENT CHINESE SONG

Itchy Dingle Dangle
Dingle Dangle Doo,
Going once!
Going twice!
Sold! To Fu Manchu!

Chorus: 卅 丰 亏 丗 九 *etc., etc.*

34

A POEM CALLED SOPHIA LOREN
OF LEEDS

Ingle Jingle
Jangle Jom
Tingle Ingle
Dangle Dom
Fringle Frangle
Bangle Bom!
And there's more, my friend,
Where that came from! !

MAN SAYING "MORE WHERE THAT CAME FROM" IN GUM ARABIC.

World's Record Talks Bubble.

THE PRAYER OF THE CIVIL SERVANT

When it's OBE time in England
And the knighthoods flow like wine,
In next year's Birthday Honours
If you're stuck for a name, use mine.

Chorus: Rule Britannia, *etc., etc.*

"There is no money. It says he's taken it with him!"

Judith Hart
  once made for me
    an early morning
      cup of tea.

It isn't every
  day that we
    are waited on
      by an MP.

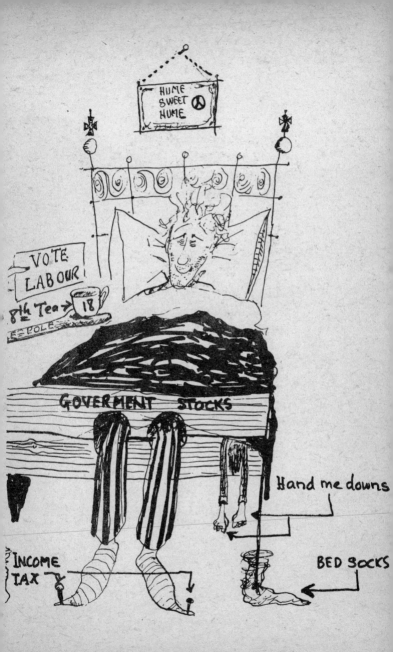

MALICE AT BUCKINGHAM PALACE

Outside Buckingham Palace
  a dog was barking one day
When out of a house
  came a chocolate mouse
And frightened that doggie away.

And so that chocolate mousie
  was taken to the Queen—
Who swallowed him up
  with a gobbledy glup.
I do think that was mean.

Chorus: Here's a health unto her Majesty, *etc., etc.*

The Blank of England

43

"I tell you, Madam, you won't see any fish this time of night."

THE SKATE

'Tis sad to relate
That skate cannot skate!
In the sea, they lie on the bottom.
They lie quite still
In waters chill
Until a fisherman's got 'em!

A very sad fate
for the non-skating skate.

Chorus: Rule Britannia, *etc., etc.*

Genuine Skating Fish

Deep-frozen Skate

EELS

Eileen Carrol
Had a barrel
Filled with writhing eels
And just for fun
She swallowed one:
Now she knows how it feels.

Chorus: Rule Britannia, *etc., etc.*

MY HAPPILY SPLASHING DAUGHTER

My happily splashing daughter
Said, "My legs are getting shorter!"
Well she must be dim
To go for a swim
In that shark-ridden water!

When I get hot
They say I've got
A temperature or flu.
If I go red ~~flu~~
I'm put to bed
With an Aspr*in*or two.
And in this state
I lie and wait
Until they *say* I'm better
Then as a rule
Sent back to School
With an explanation letter

THE DREADED TOOTSIE—KANA

When the Tootsie-Kana comes,
Hide yourself behind your thumbs;
Tie a dustbin on your head;
Stay indoors; go to bed.

When the Tootsie-Kana goes,
Peel an apple with your toes;
Buy a sausage; paint it red—
Tootsie-Kana falls down dead.

Chorus: 'Twas Blollig and the Schalomey
Touves did gear and grumble in
the Wardrobe, *etc., etc.*

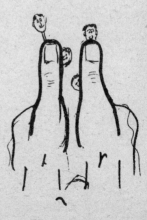

HOLY SMOKE

I am the Vicar of St Paul's
And I'm ringing the steeple bell,
The floor of the church is on fire,
Or the lid has come off hell.

Shall I ring the fire brigade?
Or should I trust in the Lord?
Oh dear! I've just remembered,
I don't think we're insured!

"What's this then?" said the fire chief.
"Is this church C of E?
It is? Then we can't put it out,
My lads are all R.C.!"

Little
Devil

"*Not only that. It also gives you lung cancer.*"

Bit Three
TWIT BITS

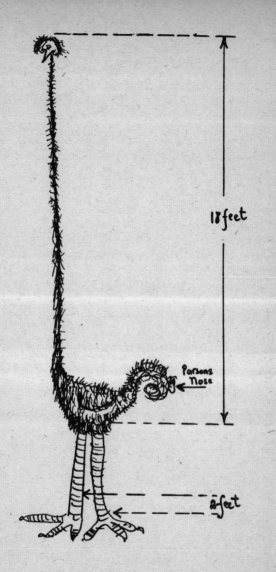

18 feet

Parsons
Nose

2 feet

Long-necked hairee

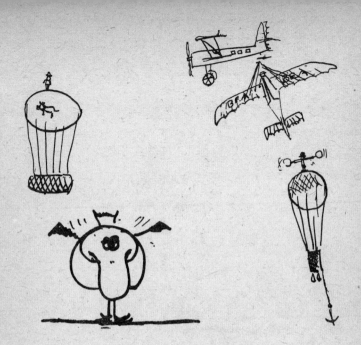

Permanently grounded flightless twitt bird
Adopted as national emblem for Concord plane project.

DUTCH HELICOPTER.

Knownothing twit birds usually seen on first nights

Little Scots-kilted hairee

Scots spider owned by Robert Bruce

SUSPICIOUS TWITT

The suspicious twitt
Has a hard time of it.
He has one major fear—
An attack from the rear!
So he perpetually revolves his head
To avoid being killed (dead).
He'll finally die a corkscrewed wreck,
Killed by a heavily twisted neck.

Chorus: Good-bye, little yellow bird, *etc., etc.*

CONTENTED LITTLE CAGED
HAIREE TWIT

A bird in a cage
Puts all heaven in a rage!
But not the contented twit,
He doesn't mind a bit.

Little Insignificant Twit

The little insignificant twit bird
Is very seldom seen or heard.
There's never been a pair, I fear,
So how the devil did he get here?

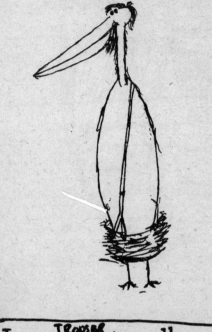

Insecure A Nesting Hairee
(TROUSER)

You've probably never heard
Of the trouser-nesting bird.
He lives on tops of houses
And wears his nest like trousers.

THE HERALDIC TWIT EAGLE

The Heraldic Twit Eagle
Is far from being regal
But he fills in the fields
On armorial shields
And during a joust
He gets hit foust.*

*First

Bit Four
SO-SO STORIES

"A month from now the BBC will be begging us to close down."

Pirates etc., on the starboard helm! That cry struck terror into the hearts, liver and kidneys of all who heard it, especially if said at sea aboard an unarmed, sinking merchantman with a cowardly crew. To story tellers is conjured up a picture of uninhibited topical highlands,* with the bones of skeletons bleached white by New Square Deal Surf! (You get eighteen per cent more bones with New Deal.) All those romantic salt-flecked days are o'er, at least I thought they were o'er until I went over to my Evening Paper and what do I see in it? Chips! Brushing them aside I finally reached the vinegar soaked columns and what do I see? Are my eyes deceiving me? Are they playing tricks? But no, there in black and white it is; but is it? It can't be, but again it is! (This is how to fill in the page folks.)

Yes, there was a pirate ship hove to off unarmed England! On board evil one-eyed men are saying Yo-ho-ho to each other. This Pirate Ship, the *Caroline* (the very name strikes terror), was beaming pop tunes with pin point accuracy at innocent unsuspecting citizens in the privacy of their own up-to-the-neck-mortgaged homes.

The G.P.O. were quick to act. Within one year they had issued a statement to the press through one of their nameless bureaucratic twits. "It is technically illegal to listen to Radio Caroline." The

* Uninhabited Tropical Islands. *Ed.*

statement set listeners by the ears. How did one know when one was listening technically or untechnically? Questions were asked in the House like:

Q: "Who was that Prime Minister I saw you with last night?"

A: "That was no Prime Minister that was Lord Home."

Finally under public pressure the Prime Monster released a statement to the Press, "No Comment." This brilliant choice of words convinced the public he was doomed in the Autumn.

Of a midnight, from Hangman's Wharf at Wapping Broadstairs, long boats with cargoes of Hit Records and Sacks of Gold, pulled out of the dock with muffled oars and muffled drums. The cargo was taken to the Island of Rockall, and buried alive. A carrier pigeon would be posted to the *Caroline* with the latest Charts marking the spot with an X, meaning the treasure was for adults only unless accompanied by a guitar playing child of sixteen. At dawn the skipper of the *Caroline*, a fiend called Captain Blackjack Jackson and Conservative member for Haiti, orders five one-legged men with eighty shovels to "dig those crazy records!" So much for the buccaneers. Now the public. What reprisals can we expect from the G.P.O. for those brave souls who dare to listen to the *Caroline*? Mr Wedgwood Benn has told me personally that we who break the law can expect "The knock on the door in the night". I have tried my best to get the election put forward to defeat this happening, and as you know, that while the Conservative Party hold a monopoly of the shareholdings in the Beatles, they will delay the day of reckoning as far as possible. By the Autumn the Beatles should be washed up, so that's what they're aiming for. Oh folks, between now and then what horrors await the "pirate listener".

Picture the scene. Midnight in the home of Mr and Mrs Eric Friggs, he a semi-humble assistant sponge lifter at Fords of Dagenham. Inside the house the blinds are drawn (but the furniture is real). The shutters are down, and the room is lit by a small candle, and a large electric light. At the back door her ear to the keyhole is the Grandmother who poses for Giles, in her hand she carries a male sock loaded with marbles. At the front window peering through the heavy curtains is the Grandfather. He is holding a World War I bayonet in a World War I hand. "All clear," he says. At this Eric Friggs pulls a heavy cupboard from the wall. Behind is a small aperture. Into this he inserts a small brass key which he keeps on a cord around his neck. A tiny door opens, revealing a small compartment, inside which is a plain white plastic Japanese transistor radio. He switches the set on, having first chosen the wavelength. There is a slight oscillation, then a brave pseudo-American voice says with great dignity "Hi there!" Here the entire family cross themselves. The voice continues, "This is the voice of Radio Caroline calling the listening free people of the World! Now here is the latest news. No. 1 in the charts: Charlie Frock and the Grovellers with

'My My Little Hairy Girl'. No. 2 and coming up fast is Grinning Frank Lapock and the Droolers with 'Ave Maria I love you'. No. 3 The Nasals with their version of 'Quo Vadis Means That I Love You'. As the records start to play the whole family twist, rock, and Madison the night away.

But outside, homing in on their illicit musical orgy are the G.P.O. detector vans. Sure enough within the hour the family are stopped in their tracks by "The knock on the door in the night". "Quick, that's a knock on the door in the night," says Gran. "Douse the light!" The Daughter snuffs the candle, the Father with speed and skill swallows the transistor set. "Right, let them in," he says. As the black leather jacketed G.P.O. men enter a scene of domestic bliss meets their gaze. The Grandmother is naked in a tin bath in front of the radiator, Grandad is reading the "Good Book" *(Fanny Hill)*, while the Son is making little plaster statues of Prince Philip making little plaster statues of the Queen. Mother is in front of the TV smoking a pipe and knitting tobacco. The G.P.O. man speaks: "We have reason to believe that you live here." Father lowers his upsidedown evening paper. "Yes, come in." His words are strangely mixed with the sound of Gerry and the Potboilers singing! Fool that he was, he'd forgotten to switch off the set before swallowing! There, dear reader, you have the picture of the horrors to come. Let the cry go up "Sink the *Caroline*!"

"Fazonki!" said Neamo Squott. The secret agent's eyes narrowed as he said the word. Not surprising— "Fazonki" in Persian means "narrow your eyes", which he in fact had instructed them to do. "No one is going to order my eyes about," he thought.

Wearing only two plastic gothic replicas of a jock strap under his beautifully tailored shantung socks, he left his room and took the lift to the Cocktail Lounge. Why he should take a lift into a Cocktail Lounge will never be known, but he, Neamo Squott, Agent 008, knew that under the floor of the lift, listening to every word was Vladinear Shotitoff, Soviet assassin by appointment to the Queen. Sitting at the door, 008 immediately disguised himself as 009. This was done by swivelling his glass eye and lowering a knee cap three inches. He ordered a Scotch on the rocks which was actually a code name for Coca Cola. Sipping it through a small lead straw he spoke. "The game's up Vladinear, come out from under that lift floor." He waited. There was no reply. Feeling under his arm Neamo produced a pearl-handled, silver-plated, Colt .45 cigarette lighter. "One more chance Vladinear. Come out or I will set fire to this secret." There came an ominous bulge, a splintering of wood, a man appeared from under the lift floor. He wore a skilful clay-work busby, and carried a small pot of cream marked U.D. One could see he was under fire.

"Good evening Neamo," he said through a Russian coxswain's megaphone.

"You saved this secret from a terrible end," replied the Englishman, returning it to its Mother.

Suddenly Vladinear tore the cap off the top of the cream and pointed it directly at Neamo.

"Don't move Englishman, this cream is curdled."

"Very well, Russian fiend, what do you want?"

Vladinear smiled. "We want to know the address of Buckingham Palace."

Neamo felt a cold feeling in his stomach, his trousers had fallen down.

"You can't fool me with that old gag," said the Russian backing towards a mouse hole. "I will count up to ten. If by thenski you have not revealed the address, I shall turn into a Peruvian dry cleaners."

At the mention of it Neamo felt the hairs at the back of his teeth stand on end.

"One," commenced the Russian, and then "two," "three, three . . . er three." A pained look appeared over Vladinear's face and he cursed his incomplete education. Neamo saw his chance. Pulling up his trousers with a trick string he handed the Russian a receipt for an albino camel called "Harods".

PULL DOWN ST. PAUL'S!

Headline in the Peking Bulletin: "English Minister of Transport buys 600 Disused Old Chinese Trams." As the Minister of Transport so wisely said at the time: "You never know, we might need them." It is in this fine tradition that we find that splendid autocrat, Sir Keith Joseph, who will for ever be remembered as the Englishman who did as much for British architecture in London as Attila did for Roman cities. Which brings us to Juxon House.

To date, all we have heard are the assinine criticisms of those who are concerned only with the west face of St. Paul's. St. Paul's indeed! Are they blind to the beauties of Juxon House? Thank heaven there are those who are not, in particular the architect, the builders, the shareholders and the owners, who are all very aware of the new jewel that is raising its clean head in Ludgate Hill.

I am glad to report that the Minister of Housing is being approached with a complaint that St. Paul's is in fact obscuring the new office block's south-west front! He will be requested to pull down part of St. Paul's to afford the public a better view of the building.

For reasons beyond logic, Sir Keith, after considering the idea, said: "While sympathising with them, the idea was financially not practicable, and it appeared that the public might be strongly averse to such a move."

In a moment of *laisser-faire*, I phoned the Ministry

and asked to speak to the Press representative. After several to eight minutes I was passed to a man called "Spokesman Said." I asked him was the Minister likely to stop the building of Juxon House?

Spokesman Said: No.

Me: Why was the plan passed in the first place?

Spokesman Said: It's very simple.

Me: I know that.

Spokesman Said: It's very simple. The building was placed in its present position for historical and commemorative reasons. Juxon House has been built on its present site because it is the identical spot on which Bishop Juxon stood to admire St. Paul's west face. That is also why the building is called Juxon House.

Me: Splendid. But did not the Minister know that public opinion was in favour of building being suspended prior to an inquiry?

Spokesman Said: Yes, but what the public did not know was that but for Sir Keith's timely intervention, St. Paul's might be no more.

Me: Exploon that. (Yes, exploon!)

Spokesman Said: The original company had plans to pull the cathedral down and build a block of self-contained St. Paul's Cathedrals.

Me: Gloria in Excelsis.

Spokesman Said: I'm sorry, that's for the Foreign Office to answer. What did you say your name was?

Me: Spokesman Listening.

Thus ended the conversation. Mulling it over in my mind, stomach, and knees, I realised if this present spate of objections continued we could get headlines like this:

L.T.E. to sue Balham Gasworks, South Face of Trolleybus Depot in Pratts Road in danger of being Obscured by new Gasometer. L.T.E. appeal to public: "Save your Balham Bus Depot from visual Vandalism."

The whole problem of obscuring will certainly divide the country in two, i.e., People versus the Government. To back up the falling prestige of the Ministry of Housing, the Government might encourage Art to abandon chiaroscuro and settle for oscuro alone. How we could see the treasures of the National Gallery presented thus is illustrated above.

But let us move forward in time and think of St. Paul's 500 years hence, that is, in another ten Sir Keith Josephs from now. Allowing that further uncontrolled building will continue in and around St. Paul's, the official tourist brochure will read like this:

Those wishing to obtain the best view of the west face should apply to the chairman of the Imprudential (whose offices stretch right across the forecourt of St. Paul's—see plan above) enclosing a five shilling postal order. You will be sent a ticket overstamped "Visitor. West Front." This entitles the holder to enter the Imprudential office block, take the lift to the seventeenth floor, where, through the window in a janitor's cupboard, a reasonable view can be had. A complete view can be obtained by photographing those areas visible from office numbers 5, 6, 7, 10, 13, 18 and 20, and piecing them together.

Owing to the heavy shadow cast by the Impru offices, it is advisable to carry a hand torch. Those who cannot afford the postal order can do it all free by following these instructions: walk to the back of the eighty-storey office block directly in front of St. Paul's: there you will find a narrow alley two feet wide; on your left will be the back of the Impru, and on your right the steps of the west face of St. Paul's; lie on your left side facing the step. Turn the head three inches to the right, at the same time craning the neck slightly to the left; cast your eyes to the extreme right and then look slightly up; now hold a small hand-mirror approximately six inches from the face, moving the mirror slowly from 45 to 60 degrees, where it will reflect a fine view of the west face. For those with money to spare the L.T.E. has laid on a special helicopter which takes up to eight passengers. Each passenger in turn is lowered between the Impru and the cathedral in a wicker basket and flown backwards and forwards along the narrow alley, allowing a panoramic view.

I think what Sir Keith Joseph had in mind was to enclose St. Paul's on all sides, thus creating a modern Petra and giving it an air of Eastern mystery.

Sir Keith sees a future in which special guides, chosen for their likeness to Sir Christopher Wren, and dressed in the costume of the period, will carry flaming brands and conduct tourists on horseback down the narrow, ink-black alleys, showing the mysterious and permanently hidden north, south, east and west fronts.

So think twice, irate citizens, ere you condemn Juxon House. As the Queen once said: "God bless Sir Keith and all who fail with him."

Exit Milligan pursued by a bear.

GIRL: Once on a time, there was a white pussy cat
and his name was Cat 'cos he went Mew! Mew!
and his tail was long. Mummy bought me a new
dress, its a Twist dress, its blue colour.

ME: Lovely, what about the pussy cat?

GIRL: Well he went for a long long walk, in the
garden, then it getted dark, God turned *alll* the
lights out, and, the pussy cat was very frightened,
very very frightened.

ME: How frightened?

GIRL: ... ... like when ... when I get mud
on the kitchen on my boots, it was Seans fault,
I don't like Sean. The mice have haded babies!

ME: How many? lots?

GIRL: No only a few lots. (Yawn)

ME: Are you sleepy?

GIRL: No only my mouth is, its cos its talking *alll*
the time.

ME: What's happened to the frightened pussy cat?

GIRL: Nothing.

ME: You left him in the dark.

GIRL: Yes he was frighted, because a bad witch
came and locked him up in her bad box.

ME: What's a bad box?

GIRL: Its a box full of bad, black bad, and the
pussy cat cried and cried and all the cry wet-ted
his leg and he catched cold, all over. The witch
went heh-heh-heh! and wouldn't stop, heh-heh-
HEH! Can witches die?

ME: Yes.

GIRL: How?

ME: They fall off their brooms. What happened to the pussy cat?

GIRL: She tooked him to her house in the forest and she said "Pussy cat, I'm going to eat your tail all up hēh-heh-heh! Den she went to bed. When she was asleep, the pussy cat—the pussy cat . . . Can the pussy cat get out of the box?

ME: I think so.

GIRL: He *climbed*-out-the-box, and he took a chopper, and Chip-Chop-Chap, he *cut* off the witches head! and she got very angry, but the pussy cat run-ned away and he lived happy ever on after.

ME: What happened to the naughty witch?

GIRL: She went to the pleese-mun and he put an ant in her knickers and then she died, and didn't have her dinner.

ME: Is that the end of the story?

GIRL: No, but I don't know any more, do you know some?

ME: No, I don't, it was *your* story, not mine.

GIRL: Was it *all* mine?

ME: Yes, I think so.

GIRL: Well I don't want any more, (Yawn).

THE END

THE HAND

There was once a great classical piano player, Plink-Plank-Plonk. His name was Claudio Vilething. He made his world debut at the Albert Hall playing Grieg's A minor piano concerto by Eileen Joyce, Plink-Plank-Plonk. Alas, came World War I, Boom-Bang-Crash. During hand to hand fighting, Wallop-Blatt-Thud, he was wounded in the hand he played the piano with, Plink-Plank-Silence.. The Doctor was jealous of Claudio's genius and said the hand would have to be amputated, Chip-Chop-Chap. After the War the Doctor gloated over the hand, Gloat-Gloat-Gloat. One night the hand lost its temper, it strangled the Doctor. And the hand lived happily ever after, Laugh-Laugh-Laugh.

Story written by hand.

"Hurry up. I'm waiting to go."

Thomas Kak winning the World Marathon straining contest with two double ruptures and a hernia.

Bit Five

DENSE JUNGLE FOR DENSE PEOPLE

Blast!

Before
venturing further
readers should now
change into a stout bush
shirt a trousers, leather
anti snake knee boots a power-
ful Solar topee a rifle. one
portable canvas Georgian Manor,
mosquitoe cream a small topical
Union Jack, three natives. The rea-
-der is now properly equipped for the
dangers that lurk in the next pa-
-ges deep in wild country on wh-
-ich no human eye has ever
set foot forward then to
dense Jingles in dense Jungles
for
Dense People

"You put your left leg in, you put your left leg out and you wave it all about."

GO NORTH, SOUTH, EAST AND WEST, YOUNG MAN

Drake is going West, lads,
So Tom is going East;
But tiny Fred
Just lies in bed,
The lazy little beast.

Chorus: Drake is going, *etc., etc.*

"Dr Beeching has gone too far, I tell you!"

Highland deer

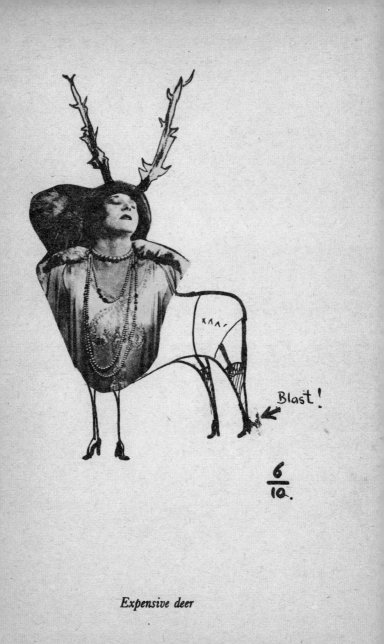

Expensive deer

THERE ONCE LIVED A VIRILE COCKEREL

There once lived a virile cockerel
With a thousand hens in Spain.
Now he's old and slow
So he'll never go
To work on an egg again.

Chorus: In Spain the rain falls, *etc., etc.*

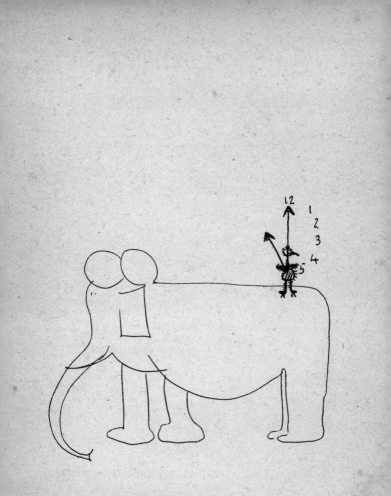

What-makes-me-tick bird

"Come on white man, show most take all."

"How did I know you were vegetarian?"

INDEX

	page
A Special Guest Appearance of Eric Sykes	15
Appearance of Eric Sykes, A Special Guest	15
Eric Sykes, A Special Guest Appearance of	15
Guest Appearance of Eric Sykes, A Special	15
Of Eric Sykes, A Special Guest Appearance	15
Special Guest Appearance of Eric Sykes, A	15
Sykes, A Special Guest Appearance of Eric	15

TANDEM BOOKS

The publishers hope that you enjoyed this book and
invite you to write for their list of other titles

UNIVERSAL-TANDEM PUBLISHING CO. LTD.
14 GLOUCESTER ROAD, LONDON SW7 4RD